The Unwritten Book

By Willy Q Friesen

Copyright © 2016 by Willy Q Friesen

The Unwritten Book
Breaking Religious Traditions
by Willy Q Friesen

Printed in the United States of America.

ISBN 9781498476911

All rights reserved solely by the author. The author guarantees all contents are original and do not infringe upon the legal rights of any other person or work. No part of this book may be reproduced in any form without the permission of the author. The views expressed in this book are not necessarily those of the publisher.

Scripture quotations taken from the New American Standard Bible (NASB). Copyright © 1960, 1962, 1963, 1968, 1971, 1972, 1973, 1975, 1977, 1995 by The Lockman Foundation. Used by permission. All rights reserved.

Scripture quotations taken from the King James Version (KJV) – *public domain*

www.xulonpress.com

Table of Contents

Author's Note ix
Introduction xi

Chapter 1: Too Much Knowledge 13
Chapter 2: Faith Unknown 17
Chapter 3: One Baptism 23
Chapter 4: Blind Faith 29
Chapter 5: Silence after Church 33
Chapter 6: Hope on Works 37
Chapter 7: Knowing too Much 43
Chapter 8: The Unforgivable Sin 47
Chapter 9: Music and the Church 51
Chapter 10: One Church 57
Chapter 11: Obediently Ignorant 61
Chapter 12: Head Covering 65
Chapter 13: Prayer 69
Chapter 14: Holy Seventh Day 75
Chapter 15: Good People 79

Foot Notes: 85

This book is dedicated to Jacob Neufeld, who originally came up with the book title, *The Unwritten Book*. He also helped title a few chapters and has given me great advice and encouragement to start and finish the book. Originally, Jacob and I were going to write this book together but work, along with other things, took most of his time away from writing and he was therefore unable to co-write it.

Author's Note

As a kid growing up in Mexico, I used to walk home from school every day and every now and then a thought would cross my mind that would scare me to the core of my soul. It was the thought of heaven and earth passing away. As I grew up I went to church about every other weekend, sometimes every week, because that was just what people did. I never really understood why I believed what I did. I remember thinking to myself, *I wish that Mexicans would all become Mennonites.* I had heard that to be able to go to heaven you had to be a Mennonite, and that the Mennonites were God's people and the rest of the world was considered worldly. I grew up going to a Mennonite church, faithfully following what they believed until I bought my first Bible. Shortly after I started reading my Bible I realized that a lot of what I had been taught was exactly the opposite from what the Bible teaches. The end result was I became a born-again Christian and got baptized a year later. Before I got baptized I asked my pastor, "Will God use me for his work?"

He told me, "If you are willing he will use you."

Now I can testify that anyone who is willing, God will use him or her in many ways.

The last chapter is written by Jake Koethler. My desire is getting the truth to the Mennonites and using the Ten Commandments as a tool to show the need for redemption.

I feel like I grew up just seeing the rules and works and not seeing that Jesus died for our sins, and that by putting our trust in him and living for him we can be saved.

It was my compulsion to have a small outreach in this way to the Mennonite community and those who have not realized the truth that is so evident in the Bible.

Although we all like to get credit for our work we do, let us not look at what the author has done or written, but let us look at who inspired the author to write, and that is our Lord and Savior Jesus Christ. To him be glory both now and forever.

Introduction

Before reading this book it would be good for the reader to understand that we were raised Mennonite and to understand what many Mennonites believe.

The founder, Menno Simons, was believed to be born in January 1496. Menno Simons was born in the Frisian town of Witmarsum (the Netherlands) and he died January 31, 1561 in Wüstenfelde, Schleswig-Holstein (Germany). He was baptized as an infant into the Catholic church and became a Catholic priest. In 1536 he started reading his Bible and found that what the church was teaching was not biblical and as he studied he realized that the Bible teaches that in order for us to receive salvation we must be born again and be baptized in the name of the Father and the Son and the Holy Spirit. On January 30, 1536 he told of his new commitment to Christ and was baptized soon after.[1]

The term *Mennonite* comes from Menno Simons' name, Mennonites. This is the Mennonites' origin. They were followers of the teachings of Menno Simons, which is the true teaching of the Bible.

Menno Simons' ministry was to expose false teaching in the church and to teach the truth about what the Bible teaches.

My name is Willy Friesen. I bought my first Bible in 2012 and shortly after I realized that what I believed was quite the opposite from what the Bible teaches. By God's grace he has saved me from false teachings and showed me the truth about what the Bible teaches. As Mennonites we generally all believe in the Bible, but unfortunately many Mennonites have very little knowledge of the Bible. This book is not to condemn anyone, but to expose false teaching and false religion and to replace them with the truth.

One final thing before reading this book: If you can, read this book with an open mind, because truth does not matter to a person if he is not willing to accept it.

Chapter 1

Too Much Knowledge

The more you know, the more you will be held accountable.

Is this really true? I've heard it being quoted to me by people who actually think that this is dangerous. However, let us look at what the Bible says about this.

Hosea 4:6, "My people are destroyed for lack of knowledge: because thou hast rejected knowledge, I will also reject thee, that thou shalt be no priest to me: seeing thou hast forgotten the law of thy God, I will also forget thy children."

It has been said that the more you know about the Bible the more you will be held accountable to God on Judgment Day. Well, yes and no. First I want to address the *yes*. If we go by that statement then there is a problem: We know too much already. We already know that there is a God and that he will judge us, so if we know that God will judge us and we do not learn his ways we are willingly ignorant. By not reading his Word we are willingly ignorant of knowing the truth and that leads to destruction, which we just read in Hosea 4:6.

Psalms 10:4, "The wicked, through the pride of his countenance, will not seek after God: God is not in all his thoughts."

We see it over and over again that man does not seek God because of sin or pride and, therefore, we were all dumb on purpose. Even through all of that, God still seeks us.

Revelation 3:20, "Behold, I stand at the door, and knock: if any man hear my voice, and open the door, I will come in to him, and will sup with him, and he with me."

God gave us the Bible so that we could gain knowledge and understanding. Let us think about it: If God knew that we could know too much from the Bible, wouldn't he have given us a smaller book than the Bible?

Timothy 2:15, "Study to shew thyself approved unto God, a workman that needeth not to be ashamed, rightly dividing the word of truth."

Scripture tells us study and learn more about who Jesus is. In fact, every time we look at the Old Testament and how the Israelites kept forgetting about God and falling into sin again, it was because of lack of knowledge of the scripture and of who God is.

In the book of Judges we see this to be one of the biggest problems we as humans face. When we do not know what the scriptures say, then we do exactly what the Israelites did in the book of Judges.

Judges 21:25, "In those days there was no king in Israel: every man did that which was right in his own eyes."

When we as humans do not have a leader over us a supreme ruler, we tend to just do what is right in our own eyes.

Just look at the United States of America and Canada. They now have become countries that have legalized gay marriages. Why? Because it is right in their own eyes.

Let's think about a little kid — a kid will only do what is right in its own eyes. If he grew up without guidance, where would that kid end up? There is a good chance it will be in prison. If we look at the big picture, if we as Christians will go to church all our lives and listen to what the preacher has to say and we get baptized but we do not read our Bibles and study God's word, then we are as a child growing up without a dad. We only do what is right in our own eyes.

2 Peter 3:18, "But grow in grace, and in the knowledge of our Lord and Saviour Jesus Christ. To him be glory both now and for ever. Amen."

If we take this for granted and we do not study God's word, how will we know right from wrong? Of course we all know murder is no good and stealing is bad and we try to follow the Ten Commandments, but Moses gave 613 commandments, so if we do not study the Scriptures how will we ever know them all?

2 Timothy 2:15, "Study to shew thyself approved unto God, a workman that needeth not to be ashamed, rightly dividing the word of truth."

Psalms 119:11, "Thy word have I hid in mine heart, that I might not sin against thee."

The only way we can know right from wrong is through the word of God and that is by studying God's word.

John 17:17, "[Jesus said] Sanctify them through thy truth: thy word is truth."

Jesus was talking to God and he knew that the word of God is truth, *the* truth, and we can never know too much.

2 Timothy 3:16, "All scripture is given by inspiration of God, and is profitable for doctrine, for reproof, for correction, for instruction in righteousness."

Now to address the *no*. The saying the more you know the more you will be held accountable only applies to people who have never heard about Jesus and the gospel. Those people have not heard of Jesus. They cannot reject him and they cannot reject the gospel. The reason why I believe this is because of what Jesus said in Luke 10.

Luke 10:12-13, "But I say unto you, that it shall be more tolerable in that day for Sodom, than for that city. Woe unto thee, Chorazin! woe unto thee, Bethsaida! for if the mighty works had been done in Tyre and Sidon, which have been done in you, they had a great while ago repented, sitting in sackcloth and ashes."

If we have heard the gospel and reject it over and over again, then the more we hear the more we will be held accountable, because now we have rejected the gospel the truth for which Jesus died so that we could have salvation,

So if we know that statement, "The more we know the more we will be held accountable," we already know too much to deny God and if we reject God and his word, then Jesus will reject us.

Luke 9:26, "For whosoever shall be ashamed of me and of my words, of him shall the Son of man be ashamed, when he shall come in his own glory, and in his Father's, and of the holy angels."

God will let us choose our own way because God does not force people to accept the truth. He gave us the gift of freewill; the choice of choosing between good and bad.

To sit in church Sunday after Sunday and listen to the gospel being preached and not accepting the word of God is like the people from Jesus' time like Jesus says in Luke 10. In the next chapter I will explain how to accept the truth and to apply it to our lives.

Chapter 2

Faith Unknown

Y ou cannot know whether you are going to heaven.
If you believe this, I want to ask a question that we should ask ourselves: Can we know for sure that we are going to hell? Are you sure? If you answered *yes* on this question, that brings me to another question: If we can know that we are going to hell, then why can't we know if we are going to heaven?

I will give an example and I think this fits rather well and will make anyone think about this statement.

-Where there is bad there is good.
-Where there is up there must be down as well.
-If something is hot there must be cold too.
-To know darkness you must know there is light.
-God created everything with an opposite.
-God created heaven and hell.

He also created everything so that we can know if it is real or not real, and when we look at the earth and everything in it we come to the conclusion that someone created it — we do not have to guess. We all know that sin is real and sin has an opposite as well — forgiveness. Simply put, Jesus is the opposite of sin. He can forgive sin. I do not mean he can forgive sin on Judgment Day, I mean he can forgive our sins today! Why would I think that?

Here's a story that we read about Jesus:

Luke 7:48, "And he said unto her, Thy sins are forgiven."

When were her sins forgiven? Right as she was speaking to Jesus.

Two verses later, he says, "Thy faith hath saved thee. Go in peace." We cannot know peace until we are free from sin and Jesus cannot lie. The Bible says:

Hebrews 13:8, "Jesus Christ the same yesterday, and to day, and for ever."

That means Jesus can forgive sins today just like he did with that woman. He did not tell her to wait until Judgment Day or until the eleventh hour. He said, "Thy sins are forgiven."

Here are some verses that tell us how we can have forgiveness for sin and ultimately be saved.

Romans 10:13, "For whosoever shall call upon the name of the Lord shall be saved."

John 1:12, "But as many as received him, to them gave he power to become the sons of God, even to them that believe on his name,"

1 John 5:13, "These things have I written unto you that believe on the name of the Son of God; that ye may know that ye have eternal life, and that ye may believe on the name of the Son of God."

Let's look at the verse that says *only* those who *believe* will know that they have eternal life, so we first have to believe. The saying that we cannot know if we are going to heaven is absolutely 100% different from what the Bible teaches!

One would say you can know if you are going to hell but you cannot know if you are going to heaven.

John 14:1-4, "Jesus said, I am going to prepare a place for you," (Who is the "you" that he is talking about?)

John 14:1-4, "Let not your heart be troubled: ye believe in God, believe also in me. In my Father's house are many mansions: if it were not so, I would have told you. I go to prepare a place for you. And if I go and prepare a place for you, I will come again, and receive you unto myself; that where I am, there ye may be also. And whither I go ye know, and the way ye know."

The "you" refers to all born again Christians.

Who are born again Christians, or what does that even mean?

John 3:5, "Jesus answered, Verily, verily, I say unto thee, Except a man be born of water and of the Spirit, he cannot enter into the kingdom of God."

How can someone get born again? We have to believe in Jesus, that he died for our sins and rose again, repent from our sins and let

Jesus take our hearts and make them new. In other words we should surrender to Jesus; repent means to turn away from sin.

John 3:16, "For God so loved the world, that he gave his only begotten Son, that whosoever believeth in him should not perish, but have everlasting life."

Here again, we can see that we can have everlasting life if we believe in Jesus, but that does not mean believe in our minds only, because the devil also believes that there is a God (James 2:19). It means we have to believe in our hearts as well just like Paul says in Romans.

Romans 10:9-10, "That if thou shalt confess with thy mouth the Lord Jesus, and shalt believe in thine heart that God hath raised him from the dead, thou shalt be saved. For with the heart man believeth unto righteousness; and with the mouth confession is made unto salvation."

Salvation comes from believing, but not just believing with our minds. We have to believe in our hearts and that comes by hearing the word of God. Only God saves us and makes us new. If we try to do good works, then we want to know if we can go to heaven, then we will never know. How do we know once we have done enough good works so we can go to heaven?

If we put our salvation into works, then the statement is true, then we will only find out when we get to heaven on Judgment Day. I would not advise that. If we trust in Jesus and He saves us from our sin then we can know today! You ask, "How will we know?" Good question. Here is how: When one gets saved the Holy Spirit enters into his body

Acts 1:8, "But ye shall receive power, after that the Holy Ghost is come upon you: and ye shall be witnesses unto me both in Jerusalem, and in all Judaea, and in Samaria, and unto the uttermost part of the earth."

First we need the Holy Spirit. How does one get the Holy Spirit? By prayer and by the laying on of a believer's hands.

John 3:5, "Jesus answered, Verily, verily, I say unto thee, Except a man be born of water and of the Spirit, he cannot enter into the kingdom of God."

Once we have the Spirit it will tell us that we are saved and that we are children of God. Without the Spirit you will never know if you will go to heaven.

Romans 8:16, "The Spirit itself beareth witness with our spirit, that we are the children of God."

Here we can see that we can know if we are children of God because the Spirit will tell our spirit that we are children of God. If we know that we are God's children then we can know if we are going to heaven or not, because why would God, who sent His Son Jesus to die on the cross for your sins and mine, do that for us so we can to go to heaven and then not let us know if we can know whether or not we are going? That would not make any since at all!

Here is the reason why that statement is believed in Mennonite and other cultures. It comes from 2 Corinthians 4:3-4 "But if our gospel be hid, it is hid to them that are lost: In whom the god of this world hath blinded the minds of them which believe not, lest the light of the glorious gospel of Christ, who is the image of God, should shine unto them."

The devil blinds our minds from the truth and then mixes half truths to make us believe a half truth so that we will not know the actual truth.

If you are not born again you will not know if you can go to heaven because the devil, the god of this world, has blinded your eyes (2 Corinthians 4:3-4). Therefore, you are stuck in unbelief. How can one get saved, then? Just follow what the Bible says.

Ephesians 2:8-9, "For by grace are ye saved through faith; and that not of yourselves: it is the gift of God: Not of works, lest any man should boast."

Only Jesus can save us, so do we have to do anything to get saved? Nope; just believe. Works will come after and that will be in a different chapter.

John 14:6, "Jesus saith unto him, I am the way, the truth, and the life: no man cometh unto the Father, but by me."

2 Corinthians 5:17, "Therefore if any man be in Christ, he is a new creature: old things are passed away; behold, all things are become new."

Many other places in the Bible tell us that we can be saved if we are in Christ.

Here is a little example of how Jesus can make someone new.

I was at a little party once and I got so drunk that I did not know where I was. I was two hours away from home, so I went on Google Maps and it led me to the motel where I was going to stay the night.

In the morning I got up and did not know how I got there until I saw my phone and I partially remembered what had happened.

After lunch I went to a party again and the people were so glad to see me there and I asked why. They said a guy named Willy from the same town you are from crashed last night and he passed away.

If it had been me, I do not think I would have been in heaven because I still did not know salvation. It struck too close that time. Two years earlier a guy named Willy Friesen from close to where I lived died in a semi crash and I was a truck driver as well. The phone calls I got that day were crazy. I believe God was warning me.

Hebrews 9:27, "And as it is appointed unto men once to die, but after this the judgment."

Salvation is a free gift, but it is priceless.

It has been years since I have had a drink of alcohol and I can only say, "Thank you, Jesus," because he made me new.

2 Corinthians 5:17, "Therefore if any man be in Christ, he is a new creature: old things are passed away; behold, all things are become new."

Chapter 3

One Baptism

What does "one baptism" mean? There is an argument saying that if someone gets baptized two times then he is going straight to hell. Why would someone believe this? Well, because that is what he has been taught.

Do I promote getting baptized more than once? No! However, neither do I say that people are going to hell if they do get baptized two times, because I have never read something like that in the Bible anywhere. We actually read just the opposite.

Acts 19:3-6

> And he said unto them, Unto what then were ye baptized? And they said, Unto John's baptism. Then said Paul, John verily baptized with the baptism of repentance, saying unto the people, that they should believe on him which should come after him, that is, on Christ Jesus. When they heard this, they were baptized in the name of the Lord Jesus. And when Paul had laid his hands upon them, the Holy Ghost came on them; and they spake with tongues, and prophesied.

Paul baptized twelve people here for the second time, "with the laying on of his hands with the baptism of the Holy Spirit not with water." If you have been baptized in the name of the Father, the Son and the Holy Spirit, then I do believe you should never get baptized again unless you were baptized as an infant. Nevertheless, if you did not receive the Holy Spirit when you got baptized, then ask your pastor to lay his hands on you and pray that you might receive the Holy Spirit. The Holy Spirit was promised to be sent when Jesus left and all believers would receive the Holy Spirit.

John 14:26, "But the Comforter, which is the Holy Ghost, whom the Father will send in my name, he shall teach you all things, and bring all things to your remembrance, whatsoever I have said unto you."

What does it mean to be baptized with the Holy Spirit? The Holy Spirit gives us power to do God's work, which he has prepared for us to do (Ephesians 2:10), and the Holy Spirit will also guide us teaching us to obey what the Bible tells us to do.

Acts 1:5, "For John truly baptized with water; but ye shall be baptized with the Holy Ghost not many days hence."

Since Jesus left the earth he sent the Holy Spirit so through the baptism of the Holy Spirit we receive power to do God's work and will. The apostles were commanded to wait for the Holy Ghost before they did any more work for Jesus.

Luke 24:49, "And, behold, I send the promise of my Father upon you: but tarry ye in the city of Jerusalem, until ye be endued with power from on high."

How can someone know if he has the Holy Spirit? The question needs to be answered with a question: Do you have the fruit if the Spirit?

Galatians 5:22-23 (NASB), "But the fruit of the Spirit is love, joy, peace, patience, kindness, goodness, faithfulness, gentleness, self-control; against such things there is no law."

I feel the need to explain this because so many people think they are Christians but have no fruit in them. Jesus said we would know them by their fruit.

Love

Love is something a person should have. Love is of the Holy Spirit, true love that is, and the love I am talking about here is love for your brother or sister or love for the sick and love for people in prison, love for your enemy. This can be best explained by a Bible verse.

1 John 4:20, "If a man say, I love God, and hateth his brother, he is a liar: for he that loveth not his brother whom he hath seen, how can he love God whom he hath not seen?"

Joy

Joy is the second fruit listed. It is part of being a believer. The joy a believer has is hard to explain. Even the thought of death does not take our joy away. Joy when we see another believer in Jesus, joy of knowing pain and sorrow will someday no longer be with us, and just a joyful heart.

John 16:24, "Hitherto have ye asked nothing in my name: ask, and ye shall receive, that your joy may be full."

Peace

We have peace about death. It is unexplainable in words, but a believer who has the Holy Spirit will have peace about death. I do not mean that a believer who has the Holy Spirit will not be afraid of dying because most will be afraid; no, the peace we have is peace about what will come after we die.

Philippians 4:7, "And the peace of God, which passeth all understanding, shall keep your hearts and minds through Christ Jesus."

Patience

Patience is something most people need even among believers. When we think of how much patience Jesus has with people it is crazy — all the war, the hunger and people who want nothing to do with Jesus, lots of people cursing Jesus, yet Jesus has patience with us. When we come to realize this, that is when we will begin to get more patience not just by being more relaxed, but with other people as well.

2 Peter 3:9 (NASB),

"The Lord is not slow about His promise, as some count slowness, but is patient toward you, not wishing for any to perish but for all to come to repentance."

Kindness

A kind person is a person to which others are drawn. Kindness is treating people with respect. It is selfless, but its reward is the love of others.

Ephesians 4:32, "And be ye kind one to another, tenderhearted, forgiving one another, even as God for Christ's sake hath forgiven you."

Goodness

Goodness is more than living an everyday life trying to get by. Goodness is helping a person in need and then doing it again the next week and the week after. The fruit of the Spirit does not wear out.

Luke 6:45, "A good man out of the good treasure of his heart bringeth forth that which is good; and an evil man out of the evil treasure of his heart bringeth forth that which is evil: for of the abundance of the heart his mouth speaketh."

Faithfulness

Faithfulness means that God and man can rely on a person who has the fruit of faithfulness. Jesus wants a faithful servant he can rely on and that is why it is one of the fruits.

Luke 16:10, "He that is faithful in that which is least is faithful also in much: and he that is unjust in the least is unjust also in much."

Gentleness

A gentle person can melt the hardest hearts because he or she is gentle in spirit.

Proverbs 15:1, "A soft answer turneth away wrath: but grievous words stir up anger."

Self-control

A person who has the Spirit will have self control. We read it over and over again that some spirits have control over human bodies, but when Jesus cast them out the people gained control of the bodies again

Mark 5:15, "And they come to Jesus, and see him that was possessed with the devil, and had the legion, sitting, and clothed, and in his right mind: and they were afraid."

The fruit of the Spirit is given to every believer when he is baptized with the Holy Spirit.

John 3:5, "Jesus answered, Verily, verily, I say unto thee, Except a man be born of water and of the Spirit, he cannot enter into the kingdom of God."

Getting baptized is so much more than just having water poured over someone's head or getting dunked under; getting baptized in the name of the Father and the Son and the Holy Ghost means we give our lives to the work Jesus planned for us. We die to ourselves like Paul said.

Galatians 2:20, "I am crucified with Christ: nevertheless I live; yet not I, but Christ liveth in me: and the life which I now live in the flesh I live by the faith of the Son of God, who loved me, and gave himself for me."

If you have been baptized as a Jehovah's Witness, Mormon, Catholic or any other religion other than Christianity, then I do believe it is a must to be baptized again, for it is a testimony that Jesus requires from us for total submission to him.

Mark 10:39, "And they said unto him, We can. And Jesus said unto them, Ye shall indeed drink of the cup that I drink of; and with the baptism that I am baptized withal shall ye be baptized."

Acts 2:38, "Then Peter said unto them, Repent, and be baptized every one of you in the name of Jesus Christ for the remission of sins, and ye shall receive the gift of the Holy Ghost."

We know that getting baptized is a command and that Jesus requires it.

What are we to look for if we have the Holy Spirit? How do I know if I have the Holy Spirit or not? I believe the first signs we will see if we have the Holy Spirit is we will have a longing for other people to get saved, which would be the first of the fruits of the Spirit, which is love. Second, we will get so convicted when we sin that we will desire to sin no longer. 1 John is a good book to read and see where we stand in our faith if we meet some qualifications of what we should see in us if we have been baptized with the Holy Spirit.

To conclude this chapter, let everyone ask themselves this question: Do I have the fruit if the Spirit?

Chapter 4

Blind Faith

Stay to that which you have been taught.

Growing up, I heard this statement a number of times and still hear it often to this day. This famous saying comes from 2 Timothy.

2 Timothy 3:14, "But continue thou in the things which thou hast learned and hast been assured of, knowing of whom thou hast learned them."

My parents knew this statement and claimed it often as I grew up and so do many Mennonites, but then they fail to read the next verse explaining why this verse was written.

Imagine a person that does not believe in God; why is that? There are a couple of reasons. One of them is they have been taught there is no God. Those people would fall under this category of "stay to that what you have been taught," because anything else is a lie. Most people realize there is a God but fail to realize who God really is.

A person may even believe in God and then have been taught to stay to that what he has been taught, but believing in God does not mean you are right with God. Let me repeat that: Believing in God does not mean you are right with God! It means you now believe as much as the devil does

James 2:19, "Thou believest that there is one God; thou doest well: the devils also believe, and tremble."

Since we believe that statement and because it comes from the Bible, let's read what the Bible says about the next part of this scripture. It comes as a hand in a glove. The saying comes directly from the Bible, but it connects to the next verse and cannot be read alone because then we miss the truth behind the true meaning.

2 Timothy 3:15 And that from a child thou hast known the holy scriptures, which are able to make thee wise unto salvation through faith which is in Christ Jesus.

All Scripture points to salvation through Jesus and that is what this scripture does as well, so we cannot pick apart one from another.

I believe this is one of the biggest lies, or should we call them "half truths" that Satan (the devil) has twisted in the Bible to deceive Mennonites. It comes right from the Bible. You see how Satan uses the Bible and gives you just half of the truth. He did the same thing with Jesus when he tempted Jesus in the wilderness.

Matthew 4:6, "And saith unto him, If thou be the Son of God, cast thyself down: for it is written, He shall give his angels charge concerning thee: and in their hands they shall bear thee up, lest at any time thou dash thy foot against a stone."

Note the devil said, "For it is written." The devil also did the same thing with Eve in the Garden of Eden.

> Genesis 3:1-6, "Now the serpent was more subtil than any beast of the field which the LORD God had made. And he said unto the woman, Yea, hath God said, Ye shall not eat of every tree of the garden? And the woman said unto the serpent, We may eat of the fruit of the trees of the garden: But of the fruit of the tree which is in the midst of the garden, God hath said, Ye shall not eat of it, neither shall ye touch it, lest ye die. And the serpent said unto the woman, Ye shall not surely die: For God doth know that in the day ye eat thereof, then your eyes shall be opened, and ye shall be as gods, knowing good and evil. And when the woman saw that the tree was good for food, and that it was pleasant to the eyes, and a tree to be desired to make one wise, she took of the fruit thereof, and did eat, and gave also unto her husband with her; and he did eat.

Satan still uses the Bible to this day to deceive people and to tempt them just like he did 6,000 years ago. What better way to deceive people than by using the Bible and only giving half truths? So we always have to ask ourselves when facing a statement or quote: Is this the full truth or just half truth?

Charles Stanley says partial obedience is always disobedience.[2]

My question then is: Is half of the truth always a lie as well?

If you were to be in a life or death situation and you had to trust someone on only a half truth, would you put your trust on that person and believe him even if it was only half truth, knowing you could die?

I think I would choose to not trust that person and find an alternative. Having that in mind, how much more should we not protect our souls from the one who can kill both body and soul?

Matthew 10:28, "And fear not them which kill the body, but are not able to kill the soul: but rather fear him which is able to destroy both soul and body in hell." If we have stayed to that what we have been taught and it was only half truth, where will it lead us?

I once prayed to God: Can you give me all the questions?

Why would I pray for that? Simple. If we don't have the questions, how will we find the answers?

Paul Harvey used to have a ministry of telling stories and he would always say, "And now the rest of the story."

We need to have the rest of the stories as well. Again, like in chapter one, God's people are destroyed for a lack of knowledge.

We should never be afraid to listen to someone else who has a different point of view on some things. Most likely the next person will have a different point of view on the same things than we do, but that does not always mean that he or she is wrong or even that either of us is wrong. Maybe that person can look in from the back door when we are still knocking at the front door. Think of it this way: If your friend has an argument with one of your other friends, each one will have truth to his side but maybe not full truth. If your one friend peels a banana from the bottom to the top, that does not mean his way is wrong (though the other friend might think so). It just means he does things differently than the other person. So when we are reading a book like this maybe we are getting the other half truth which we did not know but needed, like eating a banana. The stem is actually a good handle to hold when we eat the last bite of the banana.

To conclude, I want to urge who is reading this to be smart and ask questions like these:

Is what I believe truth?
How do I know what I believe is true?
Does what I believe match what the Bible says?
These questions and more can be answered by reading the Bible and following what the Bible says.

Chapter 5

Silence after Church

After church many people leave the gospel right at the front door of that church, and in some traditions it is often quoted, "Do not talk about Jesus after church because it is for the preachers, not for us."

As many people do, I grew up believing all kinds of weird things. As I understand it, this saying comes from when Mennonites came from Russia and they got persecuted for their faith.

I heard a story that in Russia when the Mennonites were persecuted and hated for their beliefs in Jesus, they kept a low profile. They kept silent after church and they would not talk about Jesus openly from fear of being either killed thrown into jail or beaten up. So that saying to keep quiet and not talk about Jesus openly was originally meant because of persecution, which somehow became a teaching. The Bible teaches us to talk openly about Jesus.

For instance, me and my one cousin were talking one night about how some people talk openly about Jesus. This was in the beginning of my walk with Christ and I said I liked talking about stuff like that. He said he did not and that talking about Jesus was not meant for us; it was for the preacher in church. Note that I did not know much about the Bible yet, and so I said to him, "So you mean that Jesus died on the cross for our sins for us to be quiet about it?" Then I showed him this next Bible verse, which at the time was the only verse that I knew where it was written, apart from Romans 8:28.

Luke 9:26, "For whosoever shall be ashamed of me and of my words, of him shall the Son of man be ashamed, when he shall come in his own glory, and in his Father's, and of the holy angels."

Our conversation did not last long after I said that.

Matthew 10:32-33, "Whosoever therefore shall confess me before men, him will I confess also before my Father which is in heaven. But whosoever shall deny me before men, him will I also deny before my Father which is in heaven.

The Bible teaches us to not be ashamed of Jesus and his words. We are to teach others about Jesus until the whole world knows him.

Matthew 24:14, "And this gospel of the kingdom shall be preached in all the world for a witness unto all nations; and then shall the end come."

Jesus will not come again until the Great Commission is fulfilled. How else will it be done other than by doing what Jesus commanded us to do, which is tell all the nations who Jesus is?

Matthew 28:19-20, "Go ye therefore, and teach all nations, baptizing them in the name of the Father, and of the Son, and of the Holy Ghost: Teaching them to observe all things whatsoever I have commanded you: and, lo, I am with you alway, even unto the end of the world. Amen."

There are so many other places in the Bible that teach this and my question is: How else can the whole world know about Jesus other than by us telling them about Jesus? The people will never all go to church, especially those who have not heard about Jesus.

If a person is a born again Christian, baptized in the name of the Father and the Son and the Holy Spirit, then the Bible tells us it is our job to tell all the world, because we are a royal priesthood according to 1 Peter 2:9.

Peter 2:9, "But ye are a chosen generation, a royal priesthood, an holy nation, a peculiar people; that ye should shew forth the praises of him who hath called you out of darkness into his marvelous light."

There are also other verses like Revelation 20:6, and more.

C. H. Spurgeon wrote, "Every Christian is either a missionary or an imposter." [3]

Matthew 12:30, "He that is not with me is against me; and he that gathereth not with me scattereth abroad."

We can see that what Spurgeon wrote is true, and that it should give us a fear that if we are not gathering people for Jesus then we are scattering them abroad. Going back to that saying, "Do not talk about Jesus; it is for the preachers," but for us to keep it to ourselves, how then are we gathering? If we are not gathering, then we need to ask ourselves a question: Are we born again? Because we are created for his workmanship.

Ephesians 2:10, "For we are his workmanship, created in Christ Jesus unto good works, which God hath before ordained that we should walk in them."

The conclusion that I come to is this: We need to spread the gospel to every lost person and talk about Jesus openly.

Romans 10:14-15, "How then shall they call on him in whom they have not believed? and how shall they believe in him of whom they have not heard? and how shall they hear without a preacher? And how shall they preach, except they be sent? as it is written, How beautiful are the feet of them that preach the gospel of peace, and bring glad tidings of good things!"

Chapter 6

Hope on Works

Be the best you can and hope that your good works are good enough to get you into heaven.

Many people who have gone to churches all their lives have this problem, and that is that they are taught that they have to be good to go to heaven and that requires good works. While works are a must for a Christian, they can never get us into heaven. I grew up going to church and never, not once that I remember, ever heard a preacher preach on this verse that tells us that there is no one who can do good.

Romans 3:12, "They are all gone out of the way, they are together become unprofitable; there is none that doeth good, no, not one."

Paul had done all he could for God before he got saved…or so he thought. He must have understood this verse better than anyone when he read it from the Psalms after he met Jesus on the Damascus Road.

Psalms 14:3, "They are all gone aside, they are all together become filthy: there is none that doeth good, no, not one."

Many people believe that while they are in their teen years they have to help dig seven graves until they have earned their own, but if they get married and nobody died in their single life and they never dug one grave during the time they were unmarried, then they are set free from this act.

How can anyone think that that is right? I mean, how do they know? Throughout the whole Bible I have never found anything like that anywhere. We should look and see what the Bible says about people.

Isaiah 64:6, "But we are all as an unclean thing, and all our righteousnesses are as filthy rags; and we all do fade as a leaf; and our iniquities, like the wind, have taken us away."

Anything we do is worthless. If we try to be good enough to go to heaven, our good works are as filthy rags. Why? Because we are born sinful and have no good in us. Someone would ask: What can I do to go to heaven? The answer is simple.

Titus 3:5, "Not by works of righteousness which we have done, but according to his mercy he saved us, by the washing of regeneration, and renewing of the Holy Ghost."

We see it is not by our righteousness, but by God's mercy we are saved by grace through faith (Ephesians 2:8-9).

What if someone has been good all his life and that person has a good heart for people?

Scripture makes it clear that even our hearts are unclean.

Jeremiah 17:9, "The heart is deceitful above all things, and desperately wicked: who can know it?"

Imagine two toddlers playing in a room with only one toy. How long does it take for those kids to fight over that toy?

As long as we are not saved (and by saved I mean born again) our works are as filthy rags.

Let's look at it this way: How many sins did it take for Adam and Eve to get kicked out of the Garden of Eden? That is right — only one!

How many sins have you committed? I assume more than one.

Adam and Eve probably worked and were good people, but that does not mean that they could now go to heaven because they were good people. They only committed one sin and therefore God had to force them to leave because God is holy and a holy God cannot overlook even just one sin.

The fact is that we have all sinned and are in need of a savior.

Romans 3:23, "For all have sinned, and come short of the glory of God."

For those people who still believe that their good works will get them to heaven, the only hope they have to get into heaven is false hope. I have heard it said, "Good works can't get you into heaven, but once you're save good works will keep you out of hell."

John 14:6, "Jesus saith unto him, I am the way, the truth, and the life: no man cometh unto the Father, but by me."

As we see here that only through Jesus we can get to the Father, no amount of good works will ever get us to heaven. We read that in scripture over and over again; it is only by Jesus.

John 10:9, "I am the door: by me if any man enter in, he shall be saved, and shall go in and out, and find pasture."

Acts 4:12, "Neither is there salvation in any other: for there is none other name under heaven given among men, whereby we must be saved."

Only by Jesus are we saved. It is not by works, it is by Jesus and Jesus alone! What else would He have meant when he said, "It is finished"? I believe that those words mean that Jesus had opened the door for all people to get saved. It is for all who believe; every sinner, no matter the sin anyone has committed (except the unrecoverable sin, which will be explained in a different chapter).

Ephesians 2:8-9, "For by grace are ye saved through faith; and that not of yourselves: it is the gift of God: Not of works, lest any man should boast."

It is not by hope. It is only by Jesus' blood that we are saved through faith in him; not hope or works, but by grace through faith.

Does that mean we no longer have to do good works?

Ephesians 2:10, "For we are his workmanship, created in Christ Jesus unto good works, which God hath before ordained that we should walk in them."

God has work planned for his children and we are created to do his work here on earth, but we can never get saved by our works. If we only have faith, that is dead being alone.

James 2:17, "Even so faith, if it hath not works, is dead, being alone."

Here are a few questions we should all ask ourselves:
Have I ever sinned?
How can my sins be forgiven? (1 John 1:9)
What can I do to get saved if works will not get me to heaven? (Romans 10:9-10)
How will I know whether or not that I am saved? (Romans 8:16)
What if I am not sure that I am saved? (Acts 2:38)

The answers to all these questions can be found in the Bible and in books like this one that show you how to get saved.

What if I am baptized, am I not going to heaven then?

The argument and belief is that...

"I am baptized and therefore I believe I am going to heaven." If that was the case, then why would Jesus have died?

Nowhere in the Bible does it say that if we get baptized then we are going to heaven! No, baptism is a symbol, a public confession of obedience to the Lord Jesus Christ.

"We may never be martyrs but we can die to self, to sin, to the world, to our plans and ambitions. That is the significance of baptism; we died with Christ and rose to new life." (Vance Haver)

"Baptism is faith in action." (Watchman Nee)

"A man who knows that he is saved by believing in Christ does not, when he is baptized, lift his baptism into a saving ordinance. In fact, he is the very best protester against that mistake, because he holds that he has no right to be baptized until he is saved." (Charles Spurgeon)[4]

Acts 8:36-37, "And as they went on their way, they came unto a certain water: and the eunuch said, See, here is water; what doth hinder me to be baptized? And Philip said, If thou believest with all thine heart, thou mayest. And he answered and said, I believe that Jesus Christ is the Son of God."

We see here that Phillip would not even have baptized the eunuch if eunuch had not believed that Jesus was the Son of God that was to come and take away sins. After he confessed that Jesus was Lord, then Philip baptized him.

If you have read this far through the book then you know by now that we are saved by grace through faith, not by baptism, nor by works, but by grace through faith. Getting baptized does not save you.

What if someone did not get baptized and died? Can he still go to heaven? I believe that there is a chance if he was a believer in Jesus and followed his commandments, yet we are committed to get baptized. I think about the thief on the cross. Was he baptized? No one knows, but it does not sound like he was and yet he was going to go to heaven, but only because he believed that Jesus would go to heaven and that he was God. I do believe everyone should get baptized after knowing who Jesus is and what he has done for us.

Conclusion

Our minds do not allow us to think that there is nothing we can do to get saved, especially the way the world operates and nothing of great value is free. Jesus suffered and died on the cross for your sins and mine. He came to seek and save that which was lost, he paid our sins in full, and when Jesus said, "It is finished," that is what he meant.

Here is an illustration of salvation being a free gift of God. I used this on a Mormon once because they also believe that works will get you to heaven.

Me: If I have $1,000,000 and I give it to you, can you reject it?

Lady: Yes.

Me: Are you sure? If I had that million dollars in my hand and I hand it to you, can you reject it?

Lady: Yes, I can.

Me: If I put the money into your bank account, can you still reject it?

Lady: Yes.

Me: Now, if I hand you the same money, can you accept it?

Lady: Yes, I can.

Me: If it is a gift, what do you have to do to receive the money?

Lady: Nothing. I just have to accept it.

Me: Salvation is the same thing, and here's how God offers us salvation. God says salvation is free, Ephesians 2:8-9.

Can you reject that?

Lady: Yes.

Me: God says it's already been paid for, John 3:16.

If your sins are paid for, can you do anything to pay for them again?

Lady: No.

Me: If salvation is a free gift, can you accept it?

Lady: Yes. Yes, I can.

I was able to explain it so she understood it and I hope you can understand it, too. If God already paid for your sins on the cross, all you have to do to inherit eternal life is to believe in Jesus that he died and rose again, repent (turn away from sin) and trust in Jesus, because we are saved by grace through faith.

Chapter 7

Knowing too Much

Knowing too much from the Bible is dangerous and will make you crazy. In other words, you will confused in your belief, and will start believing the wrong belief. In Low German we would say "*Ewageschouten*".

This saying, again, is quite the opposite of that what the Bible teaches and I want to explain how we should try to learn more.

2 Timothy 3:16, "All scripture is given by inspiration of God, and is profitable for doctrine, for reproof, for correction, for instruction in righteousness."

A more accurate and truthful statement would be: The more you know, the better understanding you will have, and to not be accountable on Judgment Day.

On this earth it is impossible to know too much truth. The Bible tells us God's Word is truth and that we are to learn from it.

John 17:17, "Sanctify them through thy truth: thy word is truth."

2 Peter 3:18, "But grow in grace, and in the knowledge of our Lord and Saviour Jesus Christ. To him be glory both now and for ever. Amen."

Why would an all-knowing God write a book for his people that was not good for them if they know too much from it? Why wouldn't God just write a book with less knowledge for his people and give that to them? Wouldn't that make more sense?

Matthew 7:11, "If ye then, being evil, know how to give good gifts unto your children, how much more shall your Father which is in heaven give good things to them that ask him?"

I love what Jesus says here, "How much more." I put this verse in here because God knows this is a good gift. How much more will not God give good things to them that ask him?

Remember Solomon? He asked God for wisdom to lead his people. Solomon was the smartest man on earth, other than Jesus, that has ever lived. Solomon spoke of wisdom and said knowledge is good. He wrote 3,000 proverbs and 1,005 songs

1 Kings 4:32, "And he spake three thousand proverbs: and his songs were a thousand and five."

One of his proverbs is Proverbs 1:7, "The fear of the LORD is the beginning of knowledge: but fools despise wisdom and instruction."

Knowledge is good and we can never get too much of it, so when Jesus says, "Sanctify them through thy truth," he means, "Sanctify them through the Bible," because the Bible is truth.

We can never understand God and all his ways, no matter how much truth we know.

Romans 11:33, "O the depth of the riches both of the wisdom and knowledge of God! how unsearchable are his judgments, and his ways past finding out!"

It is impossible for us to understand God or to know too much about him. I, for one, am glad of that because God would not be worth worshiping if we could know him because we would be just as smart as he is. Isn't that our problem? We, as humans, want to understand why we follow the things we do. That is very often why people start following a wrong belief, because they can understand it and it makes sense to them because it is man-based, but we are not called to understand it all. All we are called to do is trust God.

Proverbs 3:5-6, "Trust in the LORD with all thine heart; and lean not unto thine own understanding. In all thy ways acknowledge him, and he shall direct thy paths."

I do not know his name, but I heard of this guy who wrote a book and in this book he wrote, "As I became a believer in Jesus, I started walking the straight and narrow way." Soon along the road the road had a pitchfork and there was only one way he could go so he was forced to choose a way, either to the left or to the right. To the left it said, "Trust God," and to the right it said, "Please God."

As new Christians we will feel obligated to please God, but the Bible never tells us do that. The Bible teaches us to trust him with our whole heart we do not need to know everything and we do not need to understand everything either. All we need to do is trust him.

Isaiah 55:8-9, "For my thoughts are not your thoughts, neither are your ways my ways, saith the LORD. For as the heavens are higher than the earth, so are my ways higher than your ways, and my thoughts than your thoughts."

Trying to understand God is impossible, but one thing that the Bible teaches is that scripture is good for us and we can never read too much from it. Romans 11:32-36 also tells us, he is unsearchable and unfathomable. His ways are beyond our capabilities of knowing.

People are afraid of falling into something that is a wrong belief and I agree it is dangerous to step into something new and start believing something different than what we have been taught, so it is a good idea to be careful. I will be held accountable by God for everything that is written in this book if I teach something besides what the Bible teaches. In order for us to know the truth about God, we have to be transformed by the Holy Spirit so that we start thinking differently and we have to be renewed by our minds and that is what the Bible can do for us.

Romans 12:1-2, "I beseech you therefore, brethren, by the mercies of God, that ye present your bodies a living sacrifice, holy, acceptable unto God, which is your reasonable service. And be not conformed to this world: but be ye transformed by the renewing of your mind, that ye may prove what is that good, and acceptable, and perfect, will of God."

It is the will of God to transform our minds, and when people are born again by being baptized of water and the Holy Spirit like Jesus said in John chapter three, then people start thinking differently because now they have the Holy Spirit in them and the Holy Spirit changes our minds to the renewing of our minds like Romans 12:1-2 says.

1 Corinthians 3:16-17, "Know ye not that ye are the temple of God, and that the Spirit of God dwelleth in you? If any man defile the temple of God, him shall God destroy; for the temple of God is holy, which temple ye are."

These verses tell us that we are a temple of God and I believe only a born again Christian is a temple of God. With no exception, we have to be born again to become a child of God and to enter into

God's kingdom. How can we do that? By the renewing of our minds, by believing in Jesus, by reading the Bible and accepting what it says in there, and then obeying the Bible and trusting in it.

Psalms 118:8, "It is better to trust in the LORD than to put confidence in man."

Chapter 8

The Unforgivable Sin

Is murder an unforgivable sin?
Many people believe after you have killed someone you are going to hell and that there is no more forgiveness available for you, but let's we read what the Bible says about this. At the end of this chapter I will share a story of a man who had the same question as I shared the gospel with him: Is murder an unforgivable sin?

We read that King David killed one of his top soldiers, Uriah, after King David committed adultery with Uriah's wife. With that in mind, let's read the verses.

> 2 Samuel 11:14-17
> And it came to pass in the morning, that David wrote a letter to Joab, and sent it by the hand of Uriah. And he wrote in the letter, saying, Set ye Uriah in the forefront of the hottest battle, and retire ye from him, that he may be smitten, and die. And it came to pass, when Joab observed the city, that he assigned Uriah unto a place where he knew that valiant men were. And the men of the city went out, and fought with Joab: and there fell some of the people of the servants of David; and Uriah the Hittite died also.

It is an unthinkable thought for any man to think that if he were married and some man had relations with his wife and later killed him how God could forgive that man, but that is the case with King David here in this story. Yet, the Bible mentions of David that he was a man after God's own heart.

Acts 13:22, "And when he had removed him, he raised up unto them David to be their king; to whom also he gave their testimony, and said, I have found David the son of Jesse, a man after mine own heart, which shall fulfill all my will."

That does not make since in any human way! We know the reason why. The Bible tells us that God is a merciful God; he is a forgiving and loving God, not wishing that any should perish but that all should have everlasting life (2 Peter 3:9).

We all know the story about Jonah, how he went into Nineveh preaching that God would destroy that city, but did you know why he tried to run first and not preach to that city? Jonah knew that God was a merciful God and that he would forgive them. One preacher once said that Jonah hated the people of Nineveh so he did not want them saved, because then they would become his brothers and sisters in the Lord.

Jonah 4:2, "And he prayed unto the LORD, and said, I pray thee, O LORD, was not this my saying, when I was yet in my country? Therefore I fled before unto Tarshish: for I knew that thou art a gracious God, and merciful, slow to anger, and of great kindness, and repentest thee of the evil."

God is a loving God and ready to forgive every person of their sins, just like the people of Nineveh and like the thief on the cross and many other places where Jesus forgives sins.

Luke 23:43, "And Jesus said unto him, Verily I say unto thee, To day shalt thou be with me in paradise."

The question remains: Is murder an unforgivable sin? Jesus only talks about one sin that is an unforgettable sin.

Mark 3:28-29, "Verily I say unto you, All sins shall be forgiven unto the sons of men, and blasphemies wherewith soever they shall blaspheme: But he that shall blaspheme against the Holy Ghost hath never forgiveness, but is in danger of eternal damnation."

Jesus says it himself that *all sins* shall be forgiven to the sons of man, but blaspheming the Holy Spirit — there is no forgiveness for that.

What is blasphemy against the Holy Spirit? The answer I do not know exactly, but I have heard that a form of blaspheming is giving credit to the devil when the Holy Spirit should have been given credit.

When Jesus died on the cross with the two thieves, one on each side of him, the one said to Jesus, "Remember me when you go to heaven." By saying that he confessed and acknowledged his sin and that Jesus was God, able to rise from the dead.

Let's pretend you and I are having a conversation and I will ask you some questions.

Question: Have you ever stolen anything, regardless of its value?

If yes, what do you call someone who steals things? A thief! We have all stolen; it can be candy, but that is still called stealing,

Now, if you lived in Jesus' time you could have been hanging next to Jesus. Would you have acknowledged your sins and confessed them to Jesus like the thief on the cross? Sin is sin and all sin brings us to hell unless we confess and repent from it (Mark 1:15). Think about the other guy on the cross; he had the same sin, but was not willing to give up his pride. All sin leads us to hell but there is only one unforgivable sin, and that is blasphemy the Holy Spirit. David was a murderer, yet Jesus talks about him as one after his own heart.

One definition of blasphemy says, "The act or offense of speaking sacrilegiously about God or sacred things; profane talk."

Some other site says it is the act of insulting or showing contempt or lack of reverence for God, to religious or holy persons or things, or toward something considered sacred or inviolable.

Some religions consider blasphemy a religious crime.

If one were to do this to the Holy Spirit that could probably be blasphemy, though I will not state this as the only form of blasphemy. Let's remember that it is serious and though all sin is bad, blasphemy is the worst form.

I heard an example of this could be found in John 10:7-20 where Jesus talks about who he is and what he is doing and then in John 10:20, "And many of them said, He hath a devil, and is mad; why hear ye him?"

This is one way of giving the credit to the devil instead of the Holy Spirit when the Holy Spirit was the one that should have gotten credit. Many say that this is one form of blasphemy. I know that this subject is widely left open, but let's remember that there is only one unforgivable sin.

The story of repenting.

On August 10, 2015 at around 8:30 pm I was about to load grain at a farmer's. My truck was very dirty so I wrote on my door, "Jesus Is Lord." A guy named Vince asked, "What do you believe in?"

I told him, "Jesus. I'm a born again Christian."

He asked, "What does that mean?" So I explained. He asked so many questions and after I told him everything I knew, he had the most important question of all. He asked, "How can I get forgiveness of my sin?"

I told him, "Believe that Jesus died for your sins and ask him to make you new. Ask him to forgive you your sins and repent from them.

Then he asked, "What if I've killed someone in a car accident? Is that too big of a sin?"

I told him, "Absolutely not. Jesus can forgive that sin as well."

Then I gave him a Bible and he asked me, "Can you show me where I can get forgiveness of my sin?"

I showed him exactly where, 1 John 1:9 and other places. It should lie on each of our hearts the way it did with Vince: Where can I get forgiveness of my sin? As we talked I was going to write my name in the Bible and he asked, "Can you write in a Holy Bible? Is it not holy?"

That question stumped me, but God gave me the right words to say again and at the end I asked him if he would like me to pray for him and he said with a big smile, "Yes," so I prayed with him and I asked God that he would forgive Vince his sin. Vince did not want to pray out loud so I told him it was okay and he could pray quietly and that I would pray out loud. I laid my hand on him and after we were done praying he looked at me with a glow on his face and said, "You have changed me. I'm different. You changed me." Then he walked away.

I have never seen a person set free like that before so instantly. It was not me who changed him; it was Jesus. Even looking at him I could see he looked different. I marked an important verse in his Bible and this is one of many that I marked.

1 John 1:9, "If we confess our sins, he is faithful and just to forgive us our sins, and to cleanse us from all unrighteousness."

Chapter 9

Music and the Church

Is music in the church a sin?
We know that we are supposed to speak in psalms and hymns to each other and to the Lord, but is it a sin in church?

Ephesians 5:19, "Speaking to yourselves in psalms and hymns and spiritual songs, singing and making melody in your heart to the Lord."

Is it a sin to have instruments in the church? I think to answer this we will have to look at this from a different angle so we can see the big picture.

In Exodus we read that God told Moses in chapters 25-39 that he was to build the Ark of the Covenant for God and that it had to be very specific because it was going to be the place for sacrifice and worship to the Lord. With that in mind, let's see how King David moved the ark on one occasion.

1 Chronicles 13:8, "And David and all Israel played before God with all their might, and with singing, and with harps, and with psalteries, and with timbrels, and with cymbals, and with trumpets."

It would be good to read the whole chapter so that the verse is not taken out of context. David took the Ark back and as they were journeying they played with all kinds of instruments before God. Notice how it does not say, "before the Ark"?

Another account of worshiping to the Lord is found in 2nd Chronicles.

> 2 Chronicles 5:12-14
> Also the Levites which were the singers, all of them of Asaph, of Heman, of Jeduthun, with their sons and their brethren, being arrayed in white linen, having cymbals and psalteries and harps, stood at the east end of the altar, and with them an hundred and twenty priests sounding with trumpets:) It came even to pass, as the trumpeters and singers were as one, to make one sound to be heard in praising and thanking the LORD; and when they lifted up their voice with the trumpets and cymbals and instruments of musick, and praised the LORD, saying, For he is good; for his mercy endureth for ever: that then the house was filled with a cloud, even the house of the LORD; So that the priests could not stand to minister by reason of the cloud: for the glory of the LORD had filled the house of God.

Again we see lots of instruments with the singers before the Lord worshipping. God's glory filled the temple and therefore I conclude that God gets honor and glory out of singing with instruments before him.

I would recommend reading the chapter "One Church" after this one to understand what a church really is and why I believe the Bible says we should worship him in the church building with instruments as well.

Colossians 3:16, "Let the word of Christ dwell in you richly in all wisdom; teaching and admonishing one another in psalms and hymns and spiritual songs, singing with grace in your hearts to the Lord."

I have been singing regularly with a group of people at an old folks' home for over two years now and we have always used some instruments to sing, though some songs we sing A cappella. One thing I have noticed that when we sing it brings the spirit of joy to people. I will just share just one occasion, though I could write of many. We came at our regular time to go sing and as we got to the old folks' home I noticed an ambulance by the entrance and I wondered what had happened. At that moment I felt like I knew God wanted us to go sing and I knew someone would be hurting inside. The people already knew us, and as we entered I saw this one lady who was sad because her friend was being taken to the hospital. There were three nurses around her trying to calm her down, but it did not seem like it had worked, and this was an experience I will never forget. It was like I knew that God wanted me to talk to that lady and cheer her up, so I went straight to her and with a big smile I looked at her, ignoring her hurting I asked her, "Hey, how are you doing today?" I said it with excitement and smiling at her. She looked at me and it looked like I caught her completely off guard.

She looked at me, surprised to see us again, and she said, "I'm doing good. How are you?" It looked like she forgot about her pain instantly and that her friend was going to the hospital because she knew we were going to sing for her.

Music has a big influence over the whole world. Just as it can take burdens away from people, it can bring burden if it is the wrong kind of music. To show you what I mean by my story, it is best explained by a Bible verse.

1 Samuel 16:23, "And it came to pass, when the evil spirit from God was upon Saul, that David took an harp, and played with his hand: so Saul was refreshed, and was well, and the evil spirit departed from him."

Why tell this story? It is not in a church. Good question. If we understand what the church really is, then we will understand that we as people are the church; it is not the building.

Many people believe that music is a sin in the church and should not be in there, but the Bible clearly tells us we are to worship God in songs and hymns. Not only that, but he tells us to play skillfully.

Psalms 33:3, "Sing unto him a new song; play skillfully with a loud noise."

> Psalms 150:1-6
> Praise ye the LORD. Praise God in his sanctuary: praise him in the firmament of his power. Praise him for his mighty acts: praise him according to his excellent greatness. Praise him with the sound of the trumpet: praise him with the psaltery and harp. Praise him with the timbrel and dance: praise him with stringed instruments and organs. Praise him upon the loud cymbals: praise him upon the high sounding cymbals. Let every thing that hath breath praise the LORD. Praise ye the LORD.

Psalms 100:1-2, "Make a joyful noise unto the LORD, all ye lands. Serve the LORD with gladness: come before his presence with singing."

David knew that the gift of salvation deserved all the praises we can offer and one of the best ways is by singing. We can express how we feel with singing and it brings joy to our souls as well as to others. To conclude this chapter I want to leave you with a quote by Charles Spurgeon out of his book *Grace: God's Unmerited Favor*.

> God delights in the covenant, and so we are sure he will not turn back from it. It is the joy of his holy heart. He delights to do his people good. To pass over transgression, iniquity, and sin is the recreation of Jehovah. Did you ever hear of God singing? It is extraordinary that the divine one would solace himself with song, yet a prophet has thus revealed the Lord to us.[5]

Zephaniah 3:17, "The LORD thy God in the midst of thee is mighty; he will save, he will rejoice over thee with joy; he will rest in his love, he will joy over thee with singing."

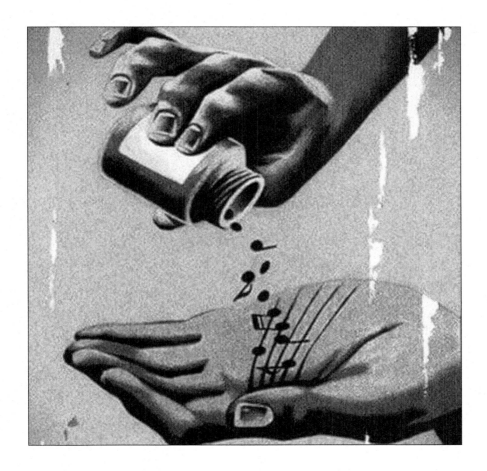

Chapter 10

One Church

In some Mennonite cultures it is strongly taught that if you are baptized you should never become a member at a different church, but stay with the one in which you were raised.

In this chapter I want to address what the church really is so that we have a fuller understanding of what it means to be baptized into Christ and be a member of the church.

Galatians 3:27-29, "For as many of you as have been baptized into Christ have put on Christ. There is neither Jew nor Greek, there is neither bond nor free, there is neither male nor female: for ye are all one in Christ Jesus. And if ye be Christ's, then are ye Abraham's seed, and heirs according to the promise.

If we are one in Christ, every born again Christian boy or girl, man or woman, Mennonite or Mexican who is baptized into Christ is now one with the rest of the believers. Jesus will someday gather the church and take them to heaven; he will not gather the churches. Let me repeat that: Jesus will not gather churches. Jesus only has one church.

Romans 12:5, "So we, being many, are one body in Christ, and every one members one of another."

> 1 Corinthians 12:12-24
> For as the body is one, and hath many members, and all the members of that one body, being many, are one body: so also is Christ. For by one Spirit are we

all baptized into one body, whether we be Jews or Gentiles, whether we be bond or free; and have been all made to drink into one Spirit. For the body is not one member, but many.

The best way I know how to explain this is to compare it to a married couple. The Bible says that once a man and a woman are married they are on longer two, but one flesh. So as Christians we become one body when we are baptized into Christ. It does not matter if the Christian is Chinese or if he comes from India, we are one body with the rest of the believers and when Jesus comes again He is coming to gather the church — his church.
Ephesians 5:25, "Husbands, love your wives, even as Christ also loved the church, and gave himself for it."
If a person is truly a born again Christian, it does not matter what church he goes to as long as they teach the truth. When two born again Christians meet they will instantly have a spiritual connection. It is like a relationship of children. A child at two years old can meet a completely different child, black or white, and they will instantly be friends because at that age they do not know the difference between races. Jesus says if we do not become like a child we will not enter into the kingdom of heaven.
I like to put things in perspective so that people can see clearly. Imagine you meet a person, not knowing his background, and you start having a conversation. You soon find out that you believe in the exact same thing. Say one year goes by and you still do not know your backgrounds but you become really good friends to the point where you would do anything for your friend. Say in the middle of a week your church leaders and another church's leaders begin arguing about their beliefs and who is right and these two churches never really saw eye-to-eye to begin with. Then you find out your good friend goes to that church. What happens? If your relationship with that friend means less than your church traditions or your church's point of view and if that friend really is a born again Christian, you are now rejecting a child of God over whose church name is better.
To really illustrate this, look at the next person. His blood runs red just like yours. His flesh was created by God just like yours and Jesus died for his sins just like yours. So where do we get the right to say he is not of the body of Christ? If you believe that your

church is better than the other church you are putting your faith in a church name, not in Jesus. If we attend an Old Colony Church, Rhinelander, EMC, EMMC, Summerfelders or any other church, the name has nothing to do with Jesus' church because Jesus' church is made up of individuals attending every kind of church — the Old Colony, Rhinelanders, EMC, EMMC, Summerfelders and many other churches. We only become a member of the true church once we are born again.

Romans 12:5, "So we, being many, are one body in Christ, and every one members one of another."

Matthew 12:30, "He that is not with me is against me; and he that gathereth not with me scattereth abroad."

Kent Hovind says it this way, "There are only two religions in this world: born again Christians and all other religions." I agree with him.

Before you come to the wrong conclusion that I would agree with an individual hopping from one church to another, I do not suggest that at all. I believe a person should help out in the church they are in and they should commit to that church if they teach the right things. Even so, to attend a different church than the one someone has been baptized in or becoming a member in a different church does not make one any less of a Christian unless he leaves the truth faith in what the church really is, because there is only one true church.

> Ephesians 1:19-23
> And what is the exceeding greatness of his power to us-ward who believe, according to the working of his mighty power, Which he wrought in Christ, when he raised him from the dead, and set him at his own right hand in the heavenly places, Far above all principality, and power, and might, and dominion, and every name that is named, not only in this world, but also in that which is to come: And hath put all things under his feet, and gave him to be the head over all things to the church, Which is his body, the fullness of him that filleth all in all.

Acts 4:12, "Neither is there salvation in any other: for there is none other name under heaven given among men, whereby we must be saved."

That means you are not saved because you are with the Old Colony, Rhinelander, EMC, EMMC, Summerfelder or any other church name. We are only saved by the name of our Lord Jesus Christ.

2 Peter 3:18, "But grow in grace, and in the knowledge of our Lord and Saviour Jesus Christ. To him be glory both now and for ever. Amen."

Chapter 11

Obediently Ignorant

The title of this chapter is written so that the whole chapter could be found in the title. Many people are obedient to churches and yet are ignorant to believe the truth. One of my close friends one time said to me, "You can read the Bible, but do not try to understand it." that day when we got into the topic of the Bible he said to me, "I believe in the Bible but I do not try to understand it because it is not for me to understand. It is only for the preachers."

I asked, "Why?"

Then he said to me, "Because it is not good for you to know too much. Your mind will start going crazy." I wish he could be convinced otherwise because he will miss most, if not all, of God's blessings.

Revelation 1:3, "Blessed is he that readeth, and they that hear the words of this prophecy, and keep those things which are written therein: for the time is at hand."

I understand where my friend is coming from because I used to be in the same belief. I did not own my own Bible until I was almost twenty-four years old, but when I started reading the Bible it was so interesting that all my spare time went into reading it. The result: I ended up giving my life to the Lord. Little did I know that the Bible contained so much knowledge for everyday life.

Acts 17:11, "These were more noble than those in Thessalonica, in that they received the word with all readiness of mind, and searched the scriptures daily, whether those things were so."

These people here in Acts searched the scriptures daily. If God did not want us to understand scripture, then why would he give us a Bible to read?" God does, on the other hand, hide scripture from people who are "willingly ignorant," not wanting to hear the truth. Kent Hovind refers to those people as, "Dumb on purpose." In other words, willingly ignorant, and that is why this chapter is titled this way.

1 Corinthians 2:14, "But the natural man receiveth not the things of the Spirit of God: for they are foolishness unto him: neither can he know them, because they are spiritually discerned."

If we are willingly ignorant, not willing to listen to the Word of God, God will hide scripture from us so that we cannot understand the scriptures. I read a book called *The Heavenly Man* about a Chinese man and he makes a statement that fits so well. He writes, "You can never really understand the scriptures until you're willing to be changed by them." [6]

Jesus knew that the people were not willing to listen to the scripture.

Luke 10:21, "In that hour Jesus rejoiced in spirit, and said, I thank thee, O Father, Lord of heaven and earth, that thou hast hid these things from the wise and prudent, and hast revealed them unto babes: even so, Father; for so it seemed good in thy sight."

King David said in Psalm 119:11, "The word have I hid in my heart that I might not sun agents thee."

David knew God's Word was truth and that it was good for a man to know.

John 17:17, "Sanctify them through thy truth: thy word is truth."

God's Word is truth and all the more we should read it and try to understand it. In fact, listen to what this verse says.

2 Timothy 3:16, "All scripture is given by inspiration of God, and is profitable for doctrine, for reproof, for correction, for instruction in righteousness."

One day, each person will stand before God and each person will have to give an account for the life which he or she lived on this earth. Before Jesus no man will be able to say, "It was because of my church," or, "Because of a preacher." Let's be ready to listen to God's Word more then to a preacher's. If all we do is listen to a preacher and not check if what he says is true then we are willingly ignorant, following a leader that could possibly be blind just like Jesus says.

Matthew 15:14, "Let them alone: they be blind leaders of the blind. And if the blind lead the blind, both shall fall into the ditch."

Following man-made religion that does not teach the Bible is like following a blind man and asking him where we should go. Here is a picture that shows how leaders can mislead if people just follow what the leaders say but do not check for themselves if what he is saying is truth.

Chapter 12

Head Covering

Is not wearing a head covering a sin?
Some people believe that not wearing a head covering is a sin for a woman and she will ultimately be going to hell if she does not start wearing one. If that is the belief then they are putting their trust in the covering instead of Jesus, and so that would be sin and the covering would more likely send them to hell then if they did not wear one.

Acts 4:12, "Neither is there salvation in any other: for there is none other name under heaven given among men, whereby we must be saved."

Let's look at it from a different angle. It is only mentioned once in the Bible that woman are to cover their heads and before reading this text I will explain a couple of things about the Bible being translated into English or any other language. In the Hebrew language they have seven different words for *love* but we in English we only have one.

In 1 Corinthians 11 we have that same problem with the word *covering* or *covered* because in the Greek language they have two different words for *covering*.

Here are the two words that we need to look at in this text: *katakalupto* and *peribolaion*. The third word, *akatakaluptos*, is just the antonym of the word *katakalupto*.

Katakalupto = cover, to cover up, to veil or cover one's self.

Akatakaluptos = unveiled, uncovered.

Peribolaion = a wrapper, mantle, veil, cloak, covering.

Now to break the words down to one word that describes each word in one word in English.

Akatakaluptos = uncovered

Katakalupto = covered

Peribolaion = covering

Now I will insert these words into the English text as they appear in the Greek language and once these words appear we will look back to what they mean.

1 Corinthians 11:1-15

Be ye followers of me, even as I also am of Christ. Now I praise you, brethren, that ye remember me in all things, and keep the ordinances, as I delivered them to you. But I would have you know, that the head of every man is Christ; and the head of the woman is the man; and the head of Christ is God. Every man praying or prophesying, having his head covered [*katakalupto* = covered], dishonoureth his head. But every woman that prayeth or prophesieth with her head uncovered [*akatakaluptos* = uncovered] dishonoureth her head: for that is even all one as if she were shaven. For if the woman be not covered [*katakalupto* = covered], let her also be shorn: but if it be a shame for a woman to be shorn or shaven, let her be covered [*Katakalupto* = covered]. For a man indeed ought not to cover [*katakalupto* = cover] his head, forasmuch as he is the image and glory of God: but the woman is the glory of the man. For the man is not of the woman; but the woman of the man. Neither was the man created for the woman; but the woman for the man. For this cause ought the woman to have power on her head because of the angels. Nevertheless neither is the man without the woman, neither the woman without the man, in the Lord. For as the woman is of the man, even so is the man also by the woman; but all things of God. Judge in yourselves: is it comely that a woman pray unto God uncovered [*akatakaluptos* = uncovered]? Doth not even nature itself teach you, that, if a man have long hair, it is a shame unto him? But if a woman have long hair, it is a glory to her: for her hair is given her for a covering [*peribolaion* = covering/veil].

The last word Paul used in verse fifteen is a completely different word in the Greek, but when translated into English the best word to use is *covering*. If we look back to the meaning of the Greek word Paul used, it means a removable veil or covering.

These next quotes are recorded shortly after Paul died, 100-200 years or so.

"So, too, did the Corinthians understand him. In fact, at this day the Corinthians do veil their virgins. What the apostles taught, their apostles approved," Tertullian (160-220 AD). [7]

K. P. Yohanan, founder of GFA (Gospel for Asia), also believes that a woman should cover her head while praying or prophesying.

When Rebecca is about to meet Isaac she covered her head and it is believed that she did it in respect of her husband-to-be

Genesis 24:64-65, "And Rebekah lifted up her eyes, and when she saw Isaac, she lighted off the camel. For she had said unto the servant, What man is this that walketh in the field to meet us? And the servant had said, It is my master: therefore she took a veil, and covered herself."

We see that it is a removable veil and that it does not constantly have to be on the head, only while praying or prophesying. Up until the year 1900 all women of every culture used head coverings; only after 1900 did this change. In my Bible study group we chose this as a topic once knowing it needed to be addressed, so we decided to study up on it. There were three of us (me and two girls) who studied this topic and surprisingly, each one of us who had studied came up with the same conclusion: It was required for women to wear a covering and for men not to while praying or prophesying. Then came the hardest part yet, because knowing about something and not applying it is, in a sense, useless. Then the question came, "Are we going to apply this now or not?" I am happy to say that the girls did start wearing one.

Regarding the people who think that this chapter is now traditional again I would like to ask you a few questions. Does your opinion overrule the Bible? Does what you want or do not want make truth less truth? Does not the Bible teach exactly what is written above? We have the Bible and we have the freedom to choose whether we will apply what is written in it or not. Dear reader, the choice is yours.

Chapter 13

Prayer

Jesus always gave thanks
As I grew up I memorized my morning prayer, my meal prayer and my prayer before I went to bed so well that I could pray and while praying I could think of all kinds of things. One day I questioned it: Is this actually praying? I knew my prayers so well that I did not even know what they meant because I would just recite them.

While I am on the subject let me say this: Saying a prayer that you have memorized and you recite or "pray" by memory is good if you think about the words that you are saying, but if someone prays and while praying is thinking about something other than the prayer, then I fully believe that that prayer is not answered. Prayer is asking God to be a part of our lives. Prayer is not reciting some words by memory.

When we pray, we should keep a few things in mind and the first thing is we should ask Jesus is to teach us to pray.

#1 Teach us how to pray.

Luke 11:1, "And it came to pass, that, as he was praying in a certain place, when he ceased, one of his disciples said unto him, Lord, teach us to pray, as John also taught his disciples."

Luke 11:1-13 tells the whole story.

#2 We are to pray in Jesus' name.

John 14:12-14, "Verily, verily, I say unto you, He that believeth on me, the works that I do shall he do also; and greater works than these shall he do; because I go unto my Father. And whatsoever ye shall ask in my name, that will I do, that the Father may be glorified in the Son. If ye shall ask any thing in my name, I will do it."

#3 We are to pray in the will of the Father.

1 John 5:14-15, "And this is the confidence that we have in him, that, if we ask any thing according to his will, he heareth us: And if we know that he hear us, whatsoever we ask, we know that we have the petitions that we desired of him."

#4 We are to pray with each other.

Matthew 18:19, "Again I say unto you, That if two of you shall agree on earth as touching any thing that they shall ask, it shall be done for them of my Father which is in heaven."

Acts 1:14, "These all continued with one accord in prayer and supplication, with the women, and Mary the mother of Jesus, and with his brethren."

#5 We are to pray in faith.

> Mark 11:23-26
> For verily I say unto you, That whosoever shall say unto this mountain, Be thou removed, and be thou cast into the sea; and shall not doubt in his heart, but shall believe that those things which he saith shall come to pass; he shall have whatsoever he saith. Therefore I say unto you, What things soever ye desire, when ye pray, believe that ye receive them, and ye shall have them. And when ye stand praying, forgive, if ye have ought against any: that your Father also which is in heaven may forgive you your trespasses. But if ye do not forgive, neither will your Father which is in heaven forgive your trespasses.

#6 We should pray expecting that prayer to be answered.

James 1:6-7, "But let him ask in faith, nothing wavering. For he that wavereth is like a wave of the sea driven with the wind and tossed. For let not that man think that he shall receive any thing of the Lord."

I believe that when we pray according to these principles (though a lot more could be said), then we know that God will answer our prayer. I want to interpret this in a way to pray as I understand prayer.

As I understand it, once we are saved we pray through the Holy Spirit who intercedes for us and brings our prayer to Jesus in a better way so that it is acceptable to Jesus (Romans 8:26), who then asks the Father for the request of his child (Romans 8:34), and when Jesus asks God for anything God will never deny Jesus of anything (Matthew 26:53). When we know God hears us, then we know we have the request for what we ask or better because the Holy Spirit brings a perfect prayer to Jesus (Romans 8:26) and Jesus goes to the Father (Romans 8:34) and when God hears our prayers he answers (1 John 5:14-15). When God speaks, we have what we need (Matthew 4:4).

Let me give an example of what happened to me while praying. On Monday, November 11, 2013, God spoke to my heart.

It is impossible to describe in words how I felt, but I will try. I had been going to baptism classes a few times already and things were new to me. My pastor at the time told me that if I ever needed prayer I should not hesitate to ask, no matter when. Early that Monday morning I went to work and at around ten o'clock in the morning my heart started to hurt — not physically, but it was as if it was longing for something very strongly. It hurt so much that I could not think about anything else. I prayed to God but it seemed like it was not helping and it felt like the more I prayed as if God wanted me to know something. I thought about calling my pastor, Ben, but he had wanted to go to Manitoba for the week and I did not want to disturb him, so I prayed some more but the pain seemed like it was just unbearable. I decided to text Pastor Ben and this is roughly what I told him.

> Good morning. I hope I'm not bothering you but could you please pray for me? My heart really hurts and I feel like God wants to tell me something but I don't know what it is, so can you pray for me? Thanks in advance.

He replied within a minute or two and said, "Good morning, Willy. Yes, I will pray right away for that."

As I received the message I laid my phone aside and started to pray and instantly my heart started feeling better and then I started to feel really happy. My heart was full of joy to the point where I did not know what to do with it all and I lifted my hands and started praising God saying, "Thank you, thank you," over and over again. Then I realized I still did not know why my heart was hurting in the first place so I asked God, "God, what does this mean? What are you trying to tell me?" At that time I opened my baptism book and each week had a memory verse and that week's verse was Matthew 4:4. As I read that verse it became clear to me what had just happened.

Matthew 4:4, "But he answered and said, It is written, Man shall not live by bread alone, but by every word that proceedeth out of the mouth of God."

It became clear as day to me that when we pray to God we receive life from God. When He speaks a word, that word is life to us. His words are what keep us alive in our every need. God wanted me to know that I can trust His Word, and the Bible is His Word.

Pastor Ben told me that Friday that as soon as he had sent that message he had started to pray and that almost immediately as he had prayed he told me that he had felt that God had answered our prayers. He said a short while after he had prayed once more for me and he said it was the same — as he started to pray he had felt strongly that God already answered our prayers.

If a person is not born again, the most important thing he can do is pray and try to find someone who knows how to pray. To explain it I will share what happened to me.

At the beginning of 2013 I was still living in sin and I was starting to look for God. One night when I was hurting beyond measure, desperate and lonely, I felt the need for someone to pray for me and I had never in my life had someone else pray for me, so I had no clue what to do or who to call, especially it being one o'clock at night. I was desperate, so I Googled a prayer line and sure enough I found one, so I called and asked if that person could pray for me. The lady on the other end of the line said, "Yes, what is it that I can pray for you about?" So I told her and she prayed a simple prayer for me, and then we hung up. My point is that if we are not born again we need help praying because we do not know how to pray.

God knows that we need prayer and that is it the most important thing we as Christians should do to have a good relationship with God.

As children of God, the God whom we call our Father, we should spend some time in prayer with Him every day and we should set aside a specific time in the day to be alone with God our Father like Jesus did.

When we pray, we should realize that prayer is a direct call to God because God has ripped the veil in half so that we ourselves can enter into the holy presence of our Lord Jesus Christ.

Jeremiah 33:3, "Call unto me, and I will answer thee, and shew thee great and mighty things, which thou knowest not."

Chapter 14

Holy Seventh Day

Exodus 20:8, "Remember the sabbath day, to keep it holy." What is the Sabbath day and when is it?

The Sabbath day is the day that God rested. He had worked six days, and the seventh day he rested.

Genesis 2:2, "And on the seventh day God ended his work which he had made; and he rested on the seventh day from all his work which he had made."

In the beginning, God created day one, then day two, then day three, then day four, then day five, then day six, and then day seven. Notice if we put them from one to seven that God worked six days and the seventh day He rested. You might think this is dumb. *Why are you explaining this? We all know how to count and seven always comes later than one!* Now with that in mind, let's look at a calendar and see what day is the last day of the week; the day God rested.

			January			
Su	Mo	Tu	We	Th	Fr	Sa
1	2	3	4	5	6	7
8	9	10	11	12	13	14
15	16	17	18	19	20	21
22	23	24	25	26	27	28
29	30	31				

The seventh day is Saturday and we have always forsaken (broken) the holy Sabbath day, which is on our Saturday, according to the calendar. Another interesting thing is that the Jews believe it is on Friday and those are God's chosen people. So are they right, or are we Christians right?

If we go by our standard calendar, then not only have we not been keeping the Sabbath day holy but we break it every week! I do believe it is good to put one day a week aside for the Lord and to rest, but let's look at what Jesus himself did and taught on the Sabbath.

Matthew 12:11-12, "And he said unto them, What man shall there be among you, that shall have one sheep, and if it fall into a pit on the sabbath day, will he not lay hold on it, and lift it out? How much then is a man better than a sheep? Wherefore it is lawful to do well on the sabbath days."

The truth is, if we want to be bound by the law (which says keep the Sabbath day holy) then we have to keep all the rest of the law as well and by that we will all fall short. Who is there that has kept the whole law, even the Ten Commandments?

Romans 6:14-15, "For sin shall not have dominion over you: for ye are not under the law, but under grace. What then? shall we sin, because we are not under the law, but under grace? God forbid."

Paul makes it clear that we are no longer under the law but under grace. That does not mean we can now do whatever we want; it just means is that on Judgment Day we will not be judged by the law. So now if we have worked on a Sunday but we are under grace, we will not be judged by the law.

> Romans 14:5-6
> One man esteemeth one day above another: another esteemeth every day alike. Let every man be fully persuaded in his own mind. He that regardeth the day, regardeth it unto the Lord; and he that regardeth not the day, to the Lord he doth not regard it. He that eateth, eateth to the Lord, for he giveth God thanks; and he that eateth not, to the Lord he eateth not, and giveth God thanks.

Paul must have known what he was talking about, because we see that even Jesus did good on the Sabbath

John 5:8-11
Jesus saith unto him, Rise, take up thy bed, and walk. And immediately the man was made whole, and took up his bed, and walked: and on the same day was the sabbath. The Jews therefore said unto him that was cured, It is the sabbath day: it is not lawful for thee to carry thy bed. He answered them, He that made me whole, the same said unto me, Take up thy bed, and walk.

John 5:17-18, "But Jesus answered them, My Father worketh hitherto, and I work. Therefore the Jews sought the more to kill him, because he not only had broken the sabbath, but said also that God was his Father, making himself equal with God."

The Jews referred to Exodus 20:8, "Remember the sabbath day, to keep it holy."

As we have already seen, Paul says that to him who keeps one day above another to the Lord, it is the same as to him who keeps every day alike to the Lord. The point of this explanation is to understand that if we serve Jesus, that is all we need to worry about. We know Jesus never committed one sin, so if he broke the Sabbath that can only mean one thing, and that is that Jesus is Lord over the Sabbath and not the Sabbath over Jesus.

I strongly believe every believer should go to church and worship God there and I do believe we should meet on different days as well.

Hebrews 10:24-25, "And let us consider one another to provoke unto love and to good works: Not forsaking the assembling of ourselves together, as the manner of some is; but exhorting one another: and so much the more, as ye see the day approaching."

Let me regard what is not keeping the Sabbath day holy. If you go out drinking on a Sunday, if you go to a restaurant on Sunday, if you turn on a water tap on a Sunday, or even just flush the toilet, then you have broken the Sabbath law because someone has to work to provide your food and water. This would now make you the master and them the slaves and that was forbidden to do by the Sabbath law.

There are also some beliefs that there are three holidays at Christmas, Easter and Pentecost and I will put this very bluntly: Jesus was not born three days in a row, Jesus did not rise for three days, and the Holy Spirit did not take three days to come down.

If you believe in the two following holidays, that they must be kept, then I have one question: Where have you read it in your Bible?

1 Peter 3:15, "But sanctify the Lord God in your hearts: and be ready always to give an answer to every man that asketh you a reason of the hope that is in you with meekness and fear."

Chapter 15

Good People

Some use the law to make us aware that we need to be saved by putting our trust in Jesus Christ.

Growing up as a Mennonite, most of us were used to hearing about heaven and hell; how we needed to do good and hope that doing enough good would outweigh the bad and there might be a hope of a possibility we would go to heaven, but not just that. Even the thought of anyone saying they would go to heaven was taboo, and saying so was a sin in itself. That is Satan's big lie for many cults and religions, to trick people into the fact that they can redeem themselves with works.

To make simple sense of what the Law (the Ten Commandments) is supposed to do and to put it plainly, it is only there to show us how sinful we are. No one can keep the Ten Commandments. We fall short, we need to be redeemed and we need to have someone pay for our sins. Why is it so hard to see what we as Mennonites already know and has been shown to most of us growing up with some knowledge of Bible stories? Jesus died on the cross for our sins, he paid for our sins, died and rose again, conquering death. Our hearts need to come to the place where we say we cannot do good enough works or do enough deeds to pay for our sins and clean our sinful hearts. We have to put our trust in the Saviour and live for him. We have to draw close to him and read and obey his Word and, yes, we are called to do good works but that is not at all what will save us. Not at all.

The Function of the law

"Just as the world was not ready for the New Testament before it received the old, just as the Jews were not prepared for the ministry of Christ until John the

Baptist had gone before Him with his call to repentance, so the unsaved are in no condition today for the gospel till the Law is applied to their hearts, because the Law is the knowledge of sin.

"It is a waste of time to sow seed on ground which has never been ploughed or spaded! To present the sacrifice of Christ to those whose passion is to take fill of sin, is to give that which is holy to the dogs," A.W. Pink. [8]

Paul persuaded sinners about Jesus using the Law of Moses. The Bible tells us that the Law is good if it is a "tutor to bring us to Christ," (Galatians 3:24). Paul wrote that he "would not have known sin except through the law," (Romans 7:7). The Law of God, the Ten Commandments, is evidently the "key of knowledge" Jesus spoke of in Luke 11:52. He was speaking to lawyers, those who should have been teaching God's Law so that sinners would receive the knowledge of sin and then see their need of the Saviour.

Prophecy speaks to the intellect of the sinner while the Law speaks to his conscience. One produces faith in the Word of God and the other brings knowledge of sin in the heart of the sinner. The Law is the God-given key to unlock the door of salvation.

"I do not believe that any man can preach the gospel who does not preach the law. The Law is the needle, and you cannot draw the silken thread of the gospel through a man's heart unless you first send the needle of the Law to make way for it," Charles Spurgeon.

Acts 28:23, "So when they had appointed him a day, many came to him at his lodging, to whom he explained and solemnly testified of the kingdom of God, persuading them concerning Jesus from both the Law of Moses and the Prophets, from morning till evening."

Notice that Paul used both prophecy and the Law of Moses in his evangelism. Prophecy appeals to a man's intellect and creates faith in the Word of God. As he realizes that the Bible is no ordinary book and that it contains numerous indisputable prophecies that prove its supernatural origin, he begins to give Scripture credibility. However, the Law of Moses appeals to a man's conscience and brings conviction of sin. A decision for Jesus in the realm of the intellect with no biblical knowledge of sin, which comes only by the Law (Romans 7:7), will almost certainly produce a false convert. The

Law's part in transformation is to make a person aware of his sin and of his need for real forgiveness and redemption and to set the standard of morality, Until a person acknowledges his basic sinfulness and inability to fulfill the demands of God's Law, he will not come repentantly to seek salvation. Until he despairs of himself and his own sinfulness, he will not come in humble faith to be filled with Christ's righteousness. A person who says he wants salvation but refuses to recognize and repent of his sin deceives himself.

"Grace means nothing to a person who does not know he is sinful and that such sinfulness means he is separated from God and damned. It is therefore pointless to preach grace until the impossible demands of the Law and the reality of guilt before God are preached," John MacArthur.

Another struggle we had as we grew up was to not read the Bible too much since it could not be understood by just anyone. To do so meant we knew too much and we would be held accountable. That we cannot know that we are saved was a thing that everyone was told.

How did we miss this and when did many of the Mennonites stop reading and believing the Gospel?

Here is another clear way to see it in scripture.

> Romans 3:19-26
> Now we know that whatever the law says, it says to those who are under the law, that every mouth may be stopped, and all the world may become guilty before God. Therefore by the deeds of the law no flesh will be justified in His sight, for by the law is the knowledge of sin.
> But now the righteousness of God apart from the law is revealed, being witnessed by the
> Law and the Prophets even the righteousness of God, through faith in Jesus Christ, to all and on all who believe. For there is no difference for all have sinned and fall short of the glory of
> God, being justified freely by His grace through the redemption that is in Christ Jesus whom God set forth as a propitiation by His blood, through faith, to demonstrate His righteousness, because in His forbearance God had passed over the sins that were

previously committed, to demonstrate at the present time His righteousness, that He might be just and the justifier of the one who has faith in Jesus.

Test yourself. Be honest. Do you think you are a good person? Have you ever told a lie, even for a good purpose? If yes, that makes you a liar. We might not like that word. We like to say we are "just human," or that we "stretched the truth." The truth is, if we have told a lie, we are liars.

Have you ever taken anything that did not belong to you, even something small? If yes, that makes you a thief. It sounds harsh, but the truth is if we have ever stolen anything, we are a thieves.

Have you ever looked at another person with lust or desire? If yes, that makes you an adulterer.

Jesus said in Matthew 5 that to look at someone with lust is to have committed adultery with that person.

Have you ever been angry with another person? Have you ever taken God's name in vain? Have you ever used God's name as a curse word or to express disgust? The Bible calls this blasphemy. According to God's standard, the Bible, that makes you a blasphemer.

You may not realize this, but those are just five of the Ten Commandments.

By your own admission and the standard of God's law, the Ten Commandments, you are a lying, thieving, blasphemous, murderous adulterer at heart. If God were to judge you by his law, would you be innocent or guilty? Be honest with yourself and God. Based on your guilty verdict, would you go to heaven or hell? The Bible says that all murderers, adulterers, thieves, and liars will have their place in the lake of fire (Revelation 21:8).

The Bible offers hope. 2 Peter 3:9 says that God is "not willing that any should perish but that all should come to repentance." Imagine you are standing in front of a judge, *guilty* of a serious crime. All the evidence has been presented and there is no doubt of your guilt. Your apologies and good works cannot erase your crimes; therefore you must be punished. The fine for your crime is $250,000 and you have no money. The judge is about to pass sentence when someone you do not even know rushes in and pays your fine for you! The court accepts the money and declares that you are free to go.

That is exactly what God did for you on the cross 2,000 years ago.

Romans 5:8, "But God commendeth his love toward us, in that, while we were yet sinners,

Christ died for us."

Jesus loved you so much that he paid the penalty for your sin so you would not have to! God has provided a way of escape, and that is through the gospel of Jesus Christ.

What must I do?

Repent of your sin. That means turning away from your sin and asking God to forgive you for breaking His law.

Jesus said in Luke 13:3, "No, I tell you! But unless you repent, you will all perish as well!"

Refuse your own self-effort. Realize that there is no way you can work your way to heaven or somehow be good enough to earn heaven.

Ephesians 2:8-9, "For by grace you are saved through faith, and this is not from yourselves, it is the gift of God; it is not from works, so that no one can boast."

Trust in Jesus Christ as your only hope. Trust in Jesus like you would trust a parachute if you were jumping out of an airplane. You would not just believe in the parachute; you would put it on and jump. That is how we must put our faith and trust in Jesus as our only hope of heaven.

Acts 4:12, "And there is salvation in no one else, for there is no other name under heaven given among people by which we must be saved."

Receive Jesus Christ as your Savior and Lord. Turn your life over to him.

John 1:12, "But as many as received Him, to them gave he power to become the sons of God, even to them that believe on His name"

Today, with all your heart, turn away from your sin and surrender your life to Jesus Christ.

Please do not put it off. You may die today and then it will be too late. Put your faith and trust in Him today.

2 Corinthians 5:17, "Therefore if any man be in Christ, he is a new creature: old things are passed away; behold, all things are become new."

Remember that the goods works and deeds you were taught are great but have no part in saving you. Good works and deeds are to be done as a result and character of being a Christian.

Foot Notes:

1, Mennonite Simon background.
https://en.m.wikipedia.org/wiki/Menno_Simons

2, Quote by Charles Stanley from his life principles Bible page 1516 copyright by Charles F Stanley copyright © 1960,1962,1963,1968,1971,1972,1973,1975,1977,1995, by THE LOCKMAN FOUNDATION LA HABRA, CA

3, Charles Spurgeon quote.
http://www.goodreads.com/author/show/2876959
Charles_Haddon_Spurgeon

4, Charles Spurgeon quote
https://www.pinterest.com/pin/5136987052031904/

5, Charles Spurgeon quote.
http://www.christianquotes.info/quotes-by-topic/quotes-about-baptism/

6, quote by Charles Spurgeon from his book Grace God's Unmerited Favor published by Whitaker House January 1 2010

7, Book: The Heavenly Man
Recorded in 2008 by Hobbit audio which owns the copyright originally published by Monarch books copyright 2002 by brother young and Paul Haddaway

8, Tertullian.
http://headcoverings.org/book-chapters/chapter04-what-early-christians-believed-about-the-head-covering

9, A.W. Pink taken from The Evidence Bible page 1338. 2011 By Ray Comfort published by Bridge-Logos Publishers Alachua, FL 32615, USA

CPSIA information can be obtained
at www.ICGtesting.com
Printed in the USA
LVOW01s1230180816
500654LV00009B/28/P